The New Arrival

The Alemany Press

Washington
Oregon
Idaho
Montana
North Dakota
South Dakota
Minnesota
Wisconsin
Michigan
Vermont
Maine
New Hampshire
Massachusetts
Rhode Island
Connecticut
New Jersey
Pennsylvania
Delaware
Maryland
West Virginia
North Carolina
South Carolina
New York
California
Nevada
Utah
Wyoming
Colorado
Nebraska
Iowa
Illinois
Indiana
Ohio
Kentucky
Virginia
Missouri
Kansas
Arizona
New Mexico
Oklahoma
Arkansas
Tennessee
Alabama
Georgia
Florida
Texas
Louisiana
Mississippi

U.S. MAP
WITH
STATE LINES

(The heavy line
indicates the area
of the first 13
states—with
present borders.)

Alaska
U.S.A.
(48 states)
Hawaii

The New Arrival

E.S.L. Stories for E.S.L. Students
Book
2

by Laurie Kuntz

Illustrated by Chan-Thou Oeur

The Alemany Press
2501 Industrial Pkwy. West,
Hayward, CA 94545

Typeset by KAZAN Typeset Services, San Francisco, CA.

ISBN: 0-88084-060-9

10 9 8 7 6 5 4

The Alemany Press
2501 Industrial Pkwy. West,
Hayward, CA 94545

Table of Contents

Acknowledgements

Special thanks to:

1. Steven DeBonis, who shared the better half.
2. Kathleen Corey, a friend, a rarity in today's world.
3. The Kuntz family, the DeBonis family and the May family, for their patience.
4. Ken & Christine Kawasaki, Audrey Nass, Lynn Savage, Dr. Barbara Robson, Erica Hagen, Mary Johnson, Dianne Walker, for encouragement, support and good ideas.
5. Roger Olsen.
6. All E.S.L. teachers working with refugees in refugee camps and at home, for caring.

Dedication

This book is dedicated to all refugees living in refugee camps; without your stories these would not exist.

Introduction

Every teacher has good and bad days. It was on one of these "bad" days, a blistering hot afternoon in Northern Thailand, that an idea germinated, which eventually grew into a book. I was teaching an advanced class of Hmong and Lao refugees at Ban-Vi-Nai camp. Though I came to class with a well prepared lesson, I could feel my students' energies waning and their attention dissipating in the torrid heat. I realized that I needed something special to grab their attention and keep it in the days to follow.

So I put the question to them. "What is it that you really want to learn? What would most interest you?"

The responses were almost all in the same vein.

"We want to read about people like ourselves, about what happens to them in America."

"We want to learn about American life."

"We want to learn about refugees who have gone to America."

Teaching E.S.L. to U.S. bound Indochinese refugees presents certain challenges not often met with in more "standard" E.S.L. situations. These people come from cultures very different from our own. Certain groups, including the people I was teaching, come from areas so remote as not to have an understanding of many of the common components of our every day life. Teaching concepts such as banking, transportation or telephones makes little sense if these are not already common objects or activities in the students' life. Culturally, this is a gap not easily bridged.

What I felt was needed was relevant reading material, through which the students could read about the experiences of someone whose life, problems and aspirations were similar to their own, whose situations were those which they had already faced or would have to face when resettled in a third country.

Nothing of this sort was available, so I decided to write a series of stories about a young Lao refugee, named Sitha.

These stories were inspired by my students' tales of their past life in Laos, their present experiences in the refugee camp and their future expectations of life in America. Because the characters and situations were pertinent they enjoyed the stories, and learning was fun again.

This book was written with the intermediate E.S.L. student in mind. It is not intended to be a grammar book. I've tried to use every day English as spoken in America. I've geared my stories to cover many of the competencies needed for day to day survivial in a new country. I think that most refugees and immigrants will be able to identify with the main character in the stories. After reading about his experiences they can say, "Yes I know how he felt. The same thing happened to me."

It's my aim to have these stories generate conversation in the classroom. After each story there is a series of student exercises and classroom activities. There are also various teaching suggestions for the teacher. These suggestions are geared to encourage student participation and group discussion, rather than having the class be teacher centered.

My aim is to present these stories in a context which all refugees can relate to. Situations actually dealing with their own experiences and needs hopefully accomplish this aim and provoke subsequent desire to learn English.

Within the E.S.L. classroom, students generally vary in language experience and ability. With this in mind, I've tried to build flexibility into the student exercises. Many of the exercises can be done on a basic level by the less advanced student or expanded upon by the more adept. This gives each student the leeway to answer and improve in accordance with his or her inclination and capacity.

Furthermore, many of the exercises lend themselves to group work. This enables the teacher to modify the exercises according to the group, if so desired. It also frees the teacher to work with particular students while the rest are active within their own groups.

There are also, in many of the exercise sections, exercises specifically for the more advanced students.

Here are several different teaching suggestions for using these stories in the classroom.

Group Readings Break the class into small groups, have each student take turns reading one or two sentences from the story while the rest listen and correct the reader's pronunciation. After all the groups have finished reading the story, the teacher then reads the story to reinforce correct pronunciation.

Vocabulary Have one student read a few sentences out loud. The other students read along and underline the words that they don't understand. The teacher then writes these words on the board and asks the class for their meaning. If no one in the class can get the meaning from the con- text of the story, teacher uses the words in another sentence. Students should try to get the meaning from the new sentences. After the meanings of all the new vocabulary words have been taught, have students create their own sentences using the new vocabulary.

Dictation Teacher uses the story as a dictation exercise. The students write the story down, then they take turns re-reading what they have written. The students then look at the original story in the book and correct their own papers. Another approach is for students to exchange and correct each other's papers

Vanishing Dialogues Teacher puts a dialogue from the book on the board. Class breaks into pairs and reads the dialogue a few times. Then the teacher erases some key words and has students fill in the blanks verbally or in writing. Teacher does this until the dialogue has completely been erased and students can say it or write it without any cue words.

Tapes Teacher tapes the story and plays it a few times for the students to hear. The students then take turns taping a portion of the story using their own words. This tape is then played back and a different student writes the taped sentences on the board. The class then corrects the sentences.

Jigsaw Listening Teacher makes three tapes of the same story, but the information on each tape is a little different (e.g. Tape one — Sitha was born in 1950, Tape two — Sitha is thirty years old, Tape three — Sitha's birthday is December 20, 1950). Class is broken into three groups. Each group listens to a different version of the story. Teacher prepares a total of at least twenty questions covering the three stories. The questions are put on the board and the students answer the questions. Some groups will not have the information to answer all of the questions, so they must listen to the other groups for the answer.

Paraphrasing The teacher reads the story to the class. Then the class must paraphrase the story in chronological order. This can be done in groups.

Telephone Teacher sends two students out of the room. A story is read to the remaining students. One student then returns and the story is related to him by the rest of the class. He, in turn, relates the story to the other student who is now called into the class. If retelling is inaccurate the teacher re-reads the story and reviews the passages that the students had difficulty with. If the class is very large, this exercise can be done in groups.

Role Playing Role playing can engender many different classroom activities. The teacher can have the students act out the whole story. Students can act out how they think the story will be resolved, or students can make up their own ending and act it out.

Rapid Speech Teacher takes one paragraph, or one sentence, at a time and reads it at a rapid pace. A student is then encouraged to repeat it. If no one is able to repeat the sentences the teacher re-reads it until the students are able to complete the exercise. Another variation is for students to write the sentences in their book and to read them back to the teacher.

The value judgements in many of these stories are not my own. They are the ideas that many of my students had about American people and the American way of life. I leave it up to the teacher to discuss the controversy in these stereotypes.

X

1

The New Arrival

Now I live in America. I'm living with a Laotian family in a small house. There are four rooms in our house. There's only one bedroom and one bathroom. There are ten people living in the house. It's crowded, but it's better than camp. This house is bigger than my house in camp.

I live in Boston. It's a big city. It's bigger than the city of Vientiane in Laos. There's a lot of traffic in Boston. It's a noisy city. It's confusing to go from one place to another. I get lost all the time.

Sometimes I miss the rice fields of Laos. I miss my small village and my family. When I think of them, I feel homesick.

There are many things that I like about Boston. I like to go to the movies and the library. There are so many books there. There are so many things to learn. In my village there was just one school. Boston has may schools. I want to study in one of them. I'd like to study English again.

There are many cheap restaurants here. I don't like American food, but there are some Chinese restaurants that I like. I'd rather eat Chinese food than American food.

When I really feel lonely, I go to the park. I like the trees and flowers there. I also like to watch the birds. The park is my favorite place here because it reminds me of my country.

Review Vocabulary

America	food
rooms	lonely
noisy	place

New Vocabulary

bedroom	restaurants
bathroom	library
room	books
Boston	park
capital	trees
city	flowers
traffic	birds
cheap	favorite

Review Verbs and Verb Phrases

live	go
miss	would like
like	would rather
buy	to remind
learn	feel
study	

New Verbs

watch

Comparatives

better
bigger

True, False, or Maybe —If the answer is True, write "T".
If the answer is False, write "F".
If the answer is Maybe, write "M".

1. Sitha lives in America. _____
2. Sitha lives alone. _____
3. This house is bigger than his house in camp. _____
4. Sitha will study again. _____
5. He'll study English. _____

Questions — Answer the following questions.
1. How many people live with Sitha?
2. Where does Sitha live?
3. Is Boston bigger than the city that you live in?
4. What does Sitha miss?
5. What does he do when he feels homesick?

For Advanced Students
1. What do you do when you feel homesick?
2. What's the title of this story? What does it mean?

Tell Me.
1. Tell me about Boston.

    a. _____

    b. _____

    c. _____

2. Tell me about the city you live in.

    a. _____

    b. _____

    c. _____

3. What do you like about your city?

    a. _____

    b. _____

    c. _____

4. What don't you like about your city?

a. _____

b. _____

c. _____

Grammar Practice — Study the following list of adjectives and their comparatives.

big — bigger	smart — smarter	young — younger
small — smaller	pretty — prettier	good — better
fast — faster	old — older	bad — worse

Now fill in the blanks of the following sentences with the comparative of the underlined adjectives.

1. My house is big.

   Your house is _____ than mine.
2. My city is small

   Your city is _____ than mine.
3. I'm smart.

   You're _____ than I am.
4. The Mekhong River is fast.

   The Charles River is _____ than the Mekhong River.
5. She's pretty.

   You're _____ than she is.
6. I'm young.

   You're _____ than I am.
7. He's a good football player.

4

   You're a _____ football player than he is.

Read the following story — Fill in each blank using the correct word.

younger — older

I'm twenty years old. My sister is thirteen years old. My brother is twenty-five years old. My sister's name is Mary, my brother's name is Henry.

Mary is my _____ sister. Henry is my _____

brother. Mary is _____ than Henry. Henry is _____

than I am.

Just for fun

Complete the following story using your own words.

My favorite place is _____. I like it because _____

When I feel _____, I go there. I _____.

Complete the following dialogue — you can do this alone or with a group of students.

Sitha: Where do you want to go today?

Nom: Let's go to _____

Sitha: _____

Nom: _____

For Advanced Students — Answer the following questions.
1. How do you feel when you're lonely?
2. What's the difference between feeling lonely and feeling homesick?
3. If you have family and friends can you still feel lonely?

2.
Different Customs

American customs are different from Laotian customs. There are many things here that I find strange and confusing.

In America, men and women often walk hand in hand. Sometimes they even kiss in public! We don't do this in Laos.

People also dress quite differently here. Very often I see women wearing shorts and sleeveless blouses. Laotian women are much too shy to dress this way.

Americans move quickly. Everyone is busy and in a hurry. People often speak in loud voices, even the women! In Laos life is slow and quiet. Maybe that's better; I don't know.

Laotians usually don't move far from their families. Here it's different. Americans often leave their families' homes at seventeen or eighteen years old!

Americans sometimes touch each other on the head! In Asia we never do that. It would be rude.

Sometimes I don't understand what's happening around me. I can't believe what I see. I think this is called culture shock.

I can't decide which culture is better. I hope things get less confusing. I know I must try to understand this new country.

Review Vocabulary

different   culture
confusing   better
also   new
around   country

New Vocabulary

customs   busy
culture shock   like
often   away
even   less
shorts   quiet
sleeveless blouse   strange
quickly   shy
hurry   loud
slow   voices
   rude

Review Verbs

walk   believe
speak   see
eat   decide
understand

New Verbs

kiss   move
dress   touch
wear   must

New expressions

hand in hand

True, False, or Maybe — If the answer is true, write "T".
     If the answer is false, write "F".
     If the answer is maybe, write "M".

1. Lao culture is different from American culture. _____
2. Laotian women wear short skirts. _____
3. Americans often speak loudly. _____
4. Every refugee or immigrant that comes to America gets culture shock. _____

Questions — Answer the following questions.
1. What are some of the things that Sitha finds strange about America?
2. Do you think Sitha likes America? Why?
3. What is culture shock?
4. Did you have culture shock?

Tell Me.

1. Tell me about Lao customs.

    a. _____

    b. _____

    c. _____

2. Tell me about American customs.

    a. _____

    b. _____

    c. _____

3. How does Sitha feel about America?

    a. _____

    b. _____

    c. _____

4. How do you feel about America?

    a. _____

    b. _____

    c. _____

5. How do people dress in your country?

    a. _____

    b. _____

    c. _____

6. What do people eat in your country?

    a. _____

    b. _____

    c. _____

Complete the following dialogue: You can do this alone or with a group of students.

Sitha meets an American. His name is Joe.

Joe: What do you think of America?

Sitha: There are many things that I like, but some things are difficult to get used to.

Joe: _____

Sitha: _____

Grammar Practice — Underline the correct verb.

1. People (dress, wear) differently in America.
2. Women (wear, dress) shorts often.
3. Lao women are too shy to (wear, dress) shorts.
4. I like to (dress, wear) in shorts and sleeveless blouses.
5. In America people (dress, wear) any way they like.

3.

Getting to Know People

When I was a small child, I was never lonely. My family was always around. My friends and I were always together. We were happy. Life was never boring. There was always a lot to do. No one was ever too busy to talk to you. I was happy to have such good friends.

Now, I live in America. When I feel homesick, I often think of my friends back in Laos. Sometimes it's lonely to live in a foreign country. There are many young people living in my neighborhood, but I don't know any of them. The Laotian family that I live with is wonderful, but I need to make my own friends. Sometimes I feel depressed.

I miss my friends in Laos. I miss Lee Pao and Chue Vue. Everyone needs friends. Everyone needs someone to talk to. I want to make new friends here in America. I hope I can make some friends soon.

Review Vocabulary		**New Vocabulary**	
child	often	never	neighborhood
boring	homesick	depressed	wonderful
busy	lonely		

Review Verbs		**New Verbs**
do	feel	talk
have	think	need
live	was, were	

10

True, False, or Maybe — If the answer is true, write "T".
If the answer is false, write "F".
If the answer is maybe, write "M".

1. In Laos Sitha was never lonely. _____
2. Sitha has many friends in America. _____
3. Sometimes Sitha is depressed. _____
4. Sitha doesn't want American friends. _____
5. There are many Lao people in Sitha's neighborhood. _____

Questions — Answer the following questions.

1. Was Sitha happy when he was a small child? Why?
2. Why does Sitha feel lonely in America?
3. Are there many foreign people in your neighborhood?
4. Where do they come from?

Tell Me.

1. Tell me about your neighborhood.

   a. _____

   b. _____

   c. _____

2. Tell me about your neighborhood in your native country.

   a. _____

   b. _____

   c. _____

Grammar Practice — Look at these words:

need (s)   want(s)   would like

There are blanks in the following story that can be filled correctly with these words. Each word will give the sentences a different meaning. Some sentences, however, will be incorrect if you're not careful to choose the right word. Fill in each blank to give the story the meaning that you want. Then see the words your classmates have used. How have they made the story different?

I have many friends. Everyone _____ friends. I'm

bored with some of my friends. I _____ to make

new friends. I _____ to make friends with people

from foreign countries.

I don't have children. I _____ to have children.

Some people feel unhappy when they don't have children.

Not me, I don't _____ children to be happy.

Use your own words to complete the following sentences.

1. Now I live in America, and _____ .

2. When I feel lonely, I _____ .

3. There are many people living in my neighborhood, and

   _____ .

4. One day I hope that _____ .

12

Just for fun

1. Think of questions that you would ask a stranger to get to know him better. Write these questions down. Now ask these questions of someone you don't know well.

   For Example
   1. Where are you from?
   2. What's your name?
   3. How long have you been here?

   1. _____

   2. _____

   3. _____

   4. _____

   5. _____

2. Describe your best friend.
3. Complete the following sentence using your own words.

   A friend is someone who _____.

4.
Buying Food

In Laos, I lived on a farm. I worked in the rice fields. My family and I had a big garden in the back of our house. We grew tomatoes, cabbages, cucumbers, onions and parsley in our garden. We had to work hard, but we were happy because we worked together.

Now that I live in Boston, I can't grow rice, I have to buy it. Boston is a big city, and there aren't any rice fields here.

Rice is sold in supermarkets and grocery stores. I shop at the big supermarket in my neighborhood. It's around the corner from my house. It has many aisles. There are different things in each aisle. Some things are in plastic bags. Others are in boxes. I can never find rice.

In the supermarket, tomatoes and cucumbers are wrapped in plastic. They look different than the ones in my garden in Laos.

It's confusing to shop in the supermarket.

Review Vocabulary

hard
neighborhood
confused

Review Verbs

	Past Tense
live	lived
work	worked
have	had
buy	grew
find	
have to	

Review Expressions

around the corner
in the back

New Vocabulary

garden	parsley
back	supermarkets
tomatoes	grocery stores
cucumbers	aisles
cabbage	plastic bags
onions	boxes

New Verbs

sell
shop
look
wrapped

15

<u>True, False, or Maybe</u> — If the answer is true, write "T".
If the answer is false, write "F".
If the answer is maybe, write "M".

1. Sitha had a rice field in the back of his house in Laos. _____
2. Sitha grows rice in Boston. _____
3. There are rice fields in Boston. _____
4. Sitha doesn't buy rice in the supermarket. _____
5. Sitha thinks it's confusing to shop in the suprmarket. _____

Questions — Answer the following questions.
1. Where was Sitha's garden?
2. What did Sitha grow in his garden?
3. Does Sitha have a garden in Boston? Why?
4. Did you have a garden in your native country? What did you grow?
5. Do you have a garden in America? What do you grow?

Grammar Review — Study the past tense of the following verbs.

live — lived	have — had
work — worked	do — did

Change the following sentences from the present tense to the past tense.
1. I live in Laos.
2. I work on a farm.
3. I have many friends.
4. Do you have a garden?

Just for fun

1. Have your class break into two teams. A person from each team will take turns playing. Your teacher will call out a letter. The person whose turn it is must think of all foods that begin with that letter. You can name fruits, vegetables, meats, fish, poultry and dairy products. You get one point for each food that your group thinks of. The group with the most points wins the game.

Example: <u>Letter M</u>

Mango	Milk
Melon	Mackerel
	Mustard, etc., etc., etc.

2. How are the following things packaged in your supermarket?

Example: rice _____

milk _____

sugar _____

apples _____

onions _____

soap _____

shampoo _____

toothpaste _____

coffee _____

tea _____

noodles _____

3. Describe how your favorite food tastes.

4. Describe the supermarket in your neighborhood.

5.
Calling a Friend

In Laos, I lived in a very small village. My friend Lek lived in Vientiane, the capital city of Laos. Vientiane was very far from my little village.

One day my cousin decided to get married. I wanted to invite Lek to the wedding, but there weren't any telephones in my village. I wrote Lek a letter. I asked him to come to my village for the wedding. I mailed the letter at the Post Office.

On the day of the wedding, I waited for Lek to arrive. I waited a long time, but he never came. The wedding was very beautiful. Everyone had a lot of fun, but I was sad because Lek never came.

Two weeks later, I finally got a letter from Lek. He wrote that he didn't get my letter until two days after the wedding! Mail was very slow in Laos. Sometimes it even got lost!

Now Lek lives in California. In America most people have telephones. It's usually easy to get in touch with people. One night I decided to call Lek on the telephone.

This is what happened:

Ring-Ring-Ring   (THE TELEPHONE IS RINGING)
A man answers.

Man:	Hello.
Sitha:	Hello, is Lek there?
Man:	You have the wrong number.
Sitha:	Sorry, I'll try again.

Sitha dials the number again.   (THE TELEPHONE RINGS)
A man answers.

Man:	Hello.
Sitha:	Hello, is Lek there?
Man:	Didn't you just call?
Sitha:	Well, uh, maybe.
Man:	Listen, you have the wrong number. Look up the right number in the phone book.
Sitha:	Excuse me, I won't call you again.

This time Sitha dials the number very carefully.
Ring-Ring-Ring (THE TELEPHONE IS RINGING)
The same man answers. (Watch out Sitha!)

Man: Hello.

Sitha: Hello, is Lek there?

Man: Listen, stupid, this is the third time you've called. You've got the wrong number! Stop bothering me!

Sitha: Excuse me, I'm sorry. I just came to this country. I'm trying to get in touch with a friend who lives in California. It's confusing to use the phone.

Man: Why don't you call the operator and ask her to help you?

Sitha: Thank you, but maybe I'll just write my friend a letter. I think it's easier!

Review Vocabulary

post office	wrong
never	one day
far	fun
right	even

Review Verbs
Past Tense

lived	wrote
was	asked
wanted	decided
had	

Review Expressions

a lot of   a long time

Review verb phrase

get married

New Vocabulary

wedding	finally
invite	first
later	most
until	operator (oper.)
beautiful	easy — easier
California	just
telephones	

New Verbs and verb phrases

call	invite
ring	mail
dial	watch out
bother	get in touch
arrive	look up
wait	

<u>True, False, or Maybe</u> — If the answer is true, write "T".

If the answer is false, write "F".

If the answer is maybe, write "M".

1. There were telephones in Sitha's village. _____
2. Sitha's letter got lost. _____
3. Everyone in America has a phone. _____
4. Sitha dialed the wrong number. _____
5. Sitha wrote his friend a letter. _____
6. Sitha doesn't like to write letters. _____

Questions — Answer the following questions.

1. Who was Sitha calling?
2. What problem did Sitha have when he tried to call Lek?
3. How many times did Sitha try to call his friend?
4. What happened when he got the wrong number?

Grammar Review — Study the past tense of the following verbs.

live — lived	mail — mailed
want — wanted	happen — happened
have to — had to	

Change the following sentences from the present tense to the past tense.

1. I live in Laos.
2. I mail letters everyday.
3. I want to make a phone call.
4. I have to call my cousin.
5. Do you want to go?
6. It happens all the time.
7. I want to study English.
8. I have to study English.

20

Complete the following dialogues:

I. Operator: Hello, may I help you?

Sitha: Yes, I _____.

Operator: _____.

Sitha: _____.

Operator: _____.

II. Information: Information, may I help you?

Sitha: Yes, I _____.

Information: _____.

Sitha: _____.

Information: _____.

Sitha: _____.

Complete the following sentences using your own words.

1. A local phone call is _____.

2. A long distance phone call is _____.

3. A long distance station to station phone call is _____.

4. A long distance person to person phone call is _____.

5. A collect phone call is _____.

6. A collect person to person phone call is _____.

7. You call Information when _____.

8. You call the operator when _____.

9. If you have a phone you must pay your _____.

10. If you don't have a phone, but want to call someone you

    can use a _____.

11. An air mail letter is _____.

12. A telegram is _____.

13. A postcard is _____.

14. The fastest way to communicate is _____.

Role Play — Pick a partner and act out the following situations:

Your child is sick and you must call the Doctor.
You want to invite a friend out to dinner.
Your house has been robbed; call the police!
You have a toothache; call the dentist.
You are calling about a job.
You are calling about an apartment for rent.

6.
Looking for a Job

It's time for me to look for a job. In Laos I was a farmer. I liked being a farmer. I like to work outdoors. I also like animals, so farming was a perfect occupation for me.

I'd like to get an interesting job in America. There are many ways to look for a job. One way is to look in the newspaper. Newspapers advertise jobs in the classified section. You can find out what jobs are available.

I bought a newspaper. It was full of jobs. "It must be easy to get a job", I thought.

Here are some of the ads that were in the newspaper.

Wanted: Mechanic to repair used cars. Call Ace Garage 123-4567 after 5 p.m.

Wanted: Females to work in a new bank as bank tellers. No experience necessary. Will train on the job. Call 567-8910 from 1 p.m.-4 p.m.

Wanted: Dishwashers in a large restaurant. Call Al, 234-5678.

I called the first number.

Sitha: Hello, I'm calling about the mechanic job advertised in the paper.

Man: Do you have experience repairing cars?

Sitha: No, I don't.

Man: Sorry, we want someone with experience.

"Well," I thought, "I might as well try again. I called the second number.

Sitha: Hello, I'm calling in reference to the bank tellers job.

Lady: Are you a woman?

Sitha: No, I'm not.

Lady: Sorry, this job is for females only.

"Well," I thought, "maybe I won't get a job today, but at least I learned a new word. I'll try again."

23

I called the third number.

Sitha: Hello, I'd like to speak to Al.
Lady: Who's calling please?
Sitha: My name is Sitha Aedavang.
Lady: What are you calling about?
Sitha: A dishwasher job.
Lady: Hold on, I'll see if Al is in.
Al: Hello, Al speaking.
Sitha: Yes, I'm calling about the dishwasher job.
Al: Do you have any experience?
Sitha: No, but I think I can do it. I need a job and I'm a
           hard worker.
Al: Okay, come for an interview tomorrow at 9 a.m.
           sharp. The address is 28 White Street.
Sitha: Thank you, see you tomorrow at 9:00 a.m.

Review Vocabulary
easy

Review Verbs

work   speak
look   need
ask   must
call   can

past tense
bought   liked
thought   wanted

New Vocabulary

occupation   full
job   perfect
worker   interesting
newspaper   sharp
classified section used
advertisement   garage
experience   females
necessary   dishwasher
reference   tomorrow
interview   address
available   dishwashing

New Verbs and Verb Phrases
look for
find out
hold on

New Verbs

advertise
repair
train

New Expression
might as well

24

<u>True, False, or Maybe</u> —If the answer is true, write "T".
If the answer is false, write "F".
If the answer is maybe, write "M".

1. Sitha was a mechanic in Laos. _____
2. Sitha likes to work outdoors. _____
3. Sitha is female. _____
4. Sitha has experience as a farmer. _____
5. Sitha will get a job as a bank teller. _____

Questions — Answer the following questions.

1. What was Sitha's occupation in Laos?
2. How many phone calls did Sitha make?
3. Is a bank teller always a woman?
4. What was the first job that Sitha asked about?
5. Would you like to be a mechanic? Why?

Tell Me.

1. Tell me about your occupation in your native country.

   a. _____

   b. _____

   c. _____

2. Tell me about your occupation in America.

   a. _____

   b. _____

Grammar Practice — Study the past tense of the following verbs:

like — liked   think — thought
call — called   buy — bought
learn — learned

Change the following sentences from the present tense to the past tense.
1. I like my job.
2. He calls about a job everyday.
3. He learns quickly.
4. I think your job is interesting.
5. He buys the newspaper every morning.

Just for fun — Answer the following questions.
1. What does a farmer do?
   Where does s/he work?
   What tools does s/he use?
2. What does a salesperson do?
   Where does s/he work?
   What tools does s/he use?
3. What does a carpenter do?
   Where does s/he work?
   What tools does s/he use?

4. What does a _____ do?

   Where does he work? _____

   What tools does he use _____

Answer the following questions.

1. If you could have any job, what job would you want? Why?
2. Is it easier for people to find a job when the live in the city or in the country?
3. What are some of the difficulties you think you'll have finding a job?
4. Make a list of women's jobs and a list of men's jobs.
   Are the women's jobs only for women? Why?
   Are the men's jobs only for men? Why?
5. The following are job advertisements from the newspaper. Read the job ads (or want ads) together with your classmates. Answer the following questions about each ad.

   1. What job is this ad for?
   2. How much is the salary?
   3. What are the requirements for the job?
   4. Do you need experience?
   5. How do you apply for the job?

BABYSITTER NEEDED
Spanish speaking in exchange for rm. and board. 555-0062.

HOUSEKEEPER/COOK
Couple seeks experienced cook/housekeeper. Excellent references required. Top salary. Send resume Box 234, Nyack N.Y 11003.

CHEF
Exp. in banquets and French cuisine. Excel. salary. Year round position. Send resume Box 100 N.Y.C. New York 10010.

PLUMBERS & HELPERS
MUST BE EXPD. Call Jerry 555-1010.

HANDYMAN (M/F)
For commercial building. Strong in electrical and plumbing. Excel. benefits. Call Mr. Martin 555-3333.

DRIVERS
Must know Brooklyn area! Own car prefrd. Top $$ Apply in person 89 Flatbush Ave. Bklyn.

MAINTENANCE CHIEF
wanted for large company. Full benefits, good salary. Call 555-6038.

SEC'Y
skilled for law firm. Dictating machine exp. pref'd. Legal exp. not required. Good salary. 555-1556.

SHIPPING CLERK
Ladies wear, Manhattan. 555-1212.

PART TIME SEC'Y
for accounting firm. 15-20 hrs. a wk. Good steno and typing. 555-0530.

7.

Getting Ready

I want to look nice for my job interview. I must wear nice clothes. I don't have fancy clothes, but my clothes are neat and clean. I don't know what to wear. It's a hard decision. Can you help me?

Help Sitha decide what to wear. Look at the following pictures. Study the new vocabulary. Choose the clothes that Sitha should wear for his job interview.

tie

long sleeved shirt

sports jacket

boots

cardigan sweater

hat

What clothes would a woman choose for her job interview?

lady's blouse

dress

skirt

lady's and men's pants

belt

coat

dress shoes

29

My interview is at 9 a.m. I'll leave my house at 8 a.m. I have to take a bus across town. I don't want to be late for my first job interview. I have the address of the restaurant, but I'm not sure where the restaurant is.

I don't have much experience traveling in the city. I hope I don't get lost. I'm nervous. It's my first job interview.

At the Restaurant

Waitress: Good morning, can I help you?
Sitha: Yes, I have an appointment with Al.
Waitress: Is this about a job?
Sitha: Yes, it is.
Waitress: You're a half hour late.
Sitha: Sorry, I got lost. I took the wrong bus.
Waitress: Al won't like that. I'll see if he's in. Take a seat please.

The Interview

Al: Hello, my name's Al Greene.

Sitha: How do you do? I'm Sitha Aedavang.

Al: Yes, your appointment was for 9 o'clock. You're late.

Sitha: Sorry, I got lost. I'm new in the city. It's difficult to find my way.

Al: If I give you a job here, you can't be late.

Sitha: Yes, I understand.

Al: How did you find out about this job?

Sitha: I saw it advertised in the paper.

Al: Do you have any experience working in a restaurant?

Sitha: No, but I'd like to try.

Al: What's your occupation?

Sitha: I was a farmer.

Al: A farmer! Where are you from?

Sitha: I'm from Laos.

Al: How much education do you have?

Sitha: Not much. You see, in my country . . .

Al: Okay, okay. Fill out this form.

The Application Form

This is the application form that Sitha has to fill out. You fill it out, too.

1. Name _____

2. Address _____

3. Telephone number _____

4. Number of dependents _____

5. Social Security Number _____

6. Date of Birth _____

7. Educational Experience — Circle the last school year completed. 1 2 3 4 5 6 7 8 9 10 11 12
   College or University — Circle the last school year completed. 1 2 3 4 5 6 7 8

8. Previous Employment Experience — List the names and addresses of your past three places of employment.

   1. _____

   2. _____

   3. _____

9. Height _____ 11. Color of eyes _____

10. Weight _____ 12. Color of hair _____

(Al looks Sitha's form over)

Al: Sorry son, there's nothing available right now.
I'll keep your application. If anything comes up,
I'll give you a call.

Sitha: Thank you, goodbye.

Review Vocabulary

look	restaurant
job interview	experience
must	city
hard	job
can	occupation
interview	sorry
A.M.	available
across	call
address	

New Vocabulary

fancy	lady's pants
clothes	long-sleeved shirt
neat	sports jacket
clean	collared sirt
late	pants
town	a tie
appointment	a belt
half hour	dress shoes
education	a cardigan
okay	a dress
form	
nervous	

Review Verbs and Verb Phrases

wear	see
help	advertise
decide	work
dress	try
take	think
hope	give
find out	look something over
have to	comes up
like	give someone a call

New Verbs and Verb Phrases

travel	take a seat
keep	find one's way
	fill out

New Expressions

right now
how do you do

<u>True, False, or Maybe</u> —If the answer is true, write "T".
If the answer is false, write "F".
If the answer is maybe, write "M".

1. It's Sitha's first job interview. _____
2. He's applying for a job as a waiter. _____
3. Sitha took the wrong bus. _____
4. Sitha's friend told him about the job. _____
5. Sitha gets the job. _____
6. Al will call him back. _____

Questions — Answer the following questions.
1. Why was Sitha nervous?
2. What time was Sitha's appointment?
3. Why was Sitha late?
4. Was Al angry at Sitha for being late?
5. Why do you think that Sitha didn't get the job?

Vocabulary Practice — Read stories 6 and 7 again. Fill in each blank with the correct expression.

take a seat	find my way
fill out	look over
comes up	look for
looking for	find out
hold on	do you do
look over	

1. Hello, how _____

2. Please, _____

3. I'm_____a job.

34

Vocabulary Practice

4. "Hello, this is Sitha calling. I'd like to speak to Jim."

   " _____ I'll see if he's home."

5. Will you please _____ this application form.

6. I'm lost. I can't _____ .

7. "Where's Jim?" "I don't know. I'll _____ him."

8. How did you _____ about this job?

9. _____ this application form, before you fill it out.

10. There's nothing now. If anything _____
    I'll call you back.

Complete the following dialogue. You can do it alone or with a group of students.

Som is applying for a job as a carpenter. He has an interview with Mr. Build.

Mr. Build: Yes, can I help you?
Som: I'd like to apply for a job as a carpenter.

Mr. Build: _____

Som: _____

Mr. Build _____

Som: _____

Just for fun

1. **Role Play** — Pick a partner. One of you is an employer and one is a person looking for a job. The employer must interview the person looking for a job.

2. You have just gotten a job. Write down some of the questions you might want to ask your employer about your new job.

   1. _____

   2. _____

   3. _____

   4. _____

   5. _____

3. You are going for a job interview. What are some of the questions the interviewer might ask you?

   1. _____

   2. _____

   3. _____

   4. _____

   5. _____

Study the new vocabulary. Choose the clothes that you'd wear when interviewing for the following jobs.

1. carpenter
2. salesgirl
3. telephone operator
4. factory worker
5. secretary
6. teacher
7. gardener
8. dishwasher

8.

A Day at the Employment Office

I wasn't having much luck finding a job from the newspaper, so I decided to try the employment office.

One morning I dressed neatly and took a bus to the employment office. This time I didn't get lost. When I got there I had to wait in line for half an hour. Finally it was my turn. A woman told me to take a seat. She was dressed in fancy clothes. She was very polite. I had to fill out a form. She looked the form over and then asked me some questions.

Woman: Where are you from?

Sitha: I'm from Laos.

Woman: What was your occupation in Laos?

Sitha: I was a farmer.

Woman: Are you employed now?

Sitha: No I'm not, but I'd like to be.

Woman: How much education do you have?

Sitha: Not much, just a few years of elementary school.

Woman: What kind of job are you looking for?

Sitha: It doesn't matter, I just want a job.

Woman: What do you have experience in?

Sitha: I can do many things well, but the only job I ever had was in farming.

Woman: Can you repair things?

Sitha: Yes, I can.

Woman: Are you interested in job training?

Sitha: Yes, I'd like that.

Woman: Can you work nights?

Sitha: Yes, I can.

Woman: Are you married?

Sitha: No, not yet.

Woman: Let me see, I'll look over my files, if anything comes up I'll give you a call.

Sitha: Thank you, goodbye.

Woman: Goodbye, Sitha. Have a nice day.

Review Vocabulary

luck	fancy
neatly	clothes
time	nice
half hour	occupation
finally	just

Review Verbs

find	repair
try	polite
dress	

Past Tense

decided   took   asked

Review Expressions

Let me see

New Vocabulary

Employment office
turn
few
elementary (elem.)
kind
files

New Expressions

it doesn't matter
not yet
job training

New verb phrase

wait in line

Exercises

True, False or Maybe — If the answer is true, write "T".
If the answer is false, write "F".
If the answer is maybe, write "M".

1. Sitha had to wait in line. _____
2. The employment office was crowded. _____
3. Sitha had to fill out a form. _____
4. The form was very difficult to fill out. _____
5. The lady in the employment office gave Sitha a job. _____

Questions

1. How did Sitha get to the employment agency?
2. How long did he have to wait in line?
3. What did Sitha have to do in the employment office?
4. Answer all of the questions that Sitha had to answer.
5. How do you think Sitha feels when he applies for a job?

Vocabulary — Complete the following sentences using your own words.

While I was waiting in line, I _____

The form I had to fill out was _____

I had to wait in line because _____

Grammar Practice — Change the following sentences into questions.

1. My interview is at 9:00 A.M.
2. I have to take a bus to the Employment Office.
3. The lady asked me many questions.
4. The questions were very difficult.

9.

English Classes

I always read the newspaper. It's a good way to learn English. I come across interesting advertisements all the time. Today I came across this one:

English as a Second Language classes to be held at Charles River Junior College: Mon.-Fri., 8 a.m. to 2 p.m., starting Jan. 11.
Classes are free of charge.
Register between Jan. 4-10 at the college, 14 River Street, Boston.

The last time I studied English was in Ban-Vi-Nai refugee camp. I think it would be a good idea to study again. I need the practice.

I decided to register. I can study during the day because I don't work yet.

I walked down to the Junior College. It wasn't far from my house. I went to the registrar's office. I had to wait in a long line. When it was my turn, I filled out an application form. In America, I'm always filling out forms and waiting in lines.

Review Vocabulary
newspaper
way
advertisement
English
classes
yet
application form
Review Verbs
read
learn
learn
study
wait in line
Past Tense
walked   filled out
had to
studied
decided
walked
went
thought
Review Expresssions
my turn

New Vocabulary
during   registrar's office
practice
course
Junior College (J.C.)

New Verbs and Verb Phrases
register
be held
start
come across,

Past Tense, came across
New Expressions
free of charge
a good idea
last time

Exercises

True, False, or Maybe — If the answer is true, write "T".
If the answer is false, write "F".
If the answer is maybe, write "M".

1. Sitha never reads the paper. _____
2. He saw an advertisement in the paper. _____
3. The classes will be held at night. _____
4. The English classes are free of charge. _____
5. Sitha is a good student. _____

Questions — Answer the following questions.

1. When is the last time Sitha studied English?
2. How did Sitha find out about the English classes?
3. Is Sitha working?
4. What did Sitha decide to do?
5. How did Sitha get to the college?
6. What did he have to do when he got there?

Vocabulary Practice — Americans use many expressions. Sometimes they are tricky. Try the following exercise. Write the expressions in the correct blanks.

last time   fill out   all the time
came across   fill in

1. She never stops talking. She talks _____ .

2. Take this form and _____ it _____ .

3. Be sure to _____ each blank.

4. I thought you had my book, but I _____ it in my room.

5. The _____ I saw you was in 1976.

10.
Student Days

There are about 25 students in my English class. They come from many different countries. About 5 students are from Cuba. There are 3 Vietnamese and 8 Cambodians. There are students from Hong Kong and Taiwan. They speak Chinese. There are also some Russian and some Haitian students.

I come from Laos. There are many ethnic groups in Laos. My ethnic group is Lao. There's another student in my class from Laos. Her ethnic group is Hmong. She speaks Hmong, but she can't speak Lao at all. We come from the same country, but we can't speak to each other. Isn't that strange?

Everyone in my class is a foreigner. They are all very friendly. We like to practice English with each other. It's a good idea to speak English all the time. After all, practice makes perfect.

My teacher is a middle-aged American woman. She's about forty-five years old. She has blue eyes and blond hair. She's an attractive lady. She's older than my teacher in the refugee camp, but she's just as friendly.

Review Vocabularly

Hmong	old–older
just	practice
strange	during
friendly	

Review Verbs
come
like

Past Tense
met

Review expressions
a good idea
at all

New Vocabulary
about
ethnic group
eyes
hair
blue
blonde
attractive
Cuba — Cubans
Vietnam — Vietnamese
Cambodia — Cambodians
Hong Kong — Chinese
Taiwan — Chinese
Laos — Laotians

New expressions
all the time
after all
practice makes perfect
middlge-aged

True, False, or Maybe — If the answer is true, write "T".
If the answer is false, write "F".
If the answer is maybe, write "M".

1. All the students in Sitha's class are from Southeast Asia. __
2. All the students can speak a little English. _____
3. Hmongs are from Laos. _____
4. The classroom is very large. _____
5. Sitha's teacher is married. _____

Tell Me.

1. How many students are in Sitha's class?
2. What countries do the other students come from?
3. What's an ethnic group?
4. What language do Cubans speak? Vietnamese? Haitians?
5. How do you think Sitha feels about being a student again? How do you fell about being a student?

Tell Me.

1. Tell me about Sitha's classmates.

    a. _____

    b. _____

    c. _____

2. Tell me about your classmates.

    a. _____

    b. _____

    c. _____

Grammar Practice — Change the words around to make the following sentences correct.

1. about students twenty five my class English in are there.
2. countries come different from many they.
3. all after, practice perfect makes.
4. like practice to English we with other each.

Vocabulary Practice — Fill in each blank with the correct expression.

all the time   after all
practice makes perfect   a good idea
wait in line   it doesn't matter
of course   not yet

1. If you want to learn English you must speak it _____.

2. There are many people here, you have to _____.

3. What do you want to eat? _____ to me.

4. Are you happy? _____ I am.

5. Are you ready? No, _____.

6. You must be tired, _____ you didn't sleep last night.

7. Speak English all the time. After all, _____.

8. Do you want to study English? Yes, I think it's _____.

Just for fun
1. Describe your teacher.
2. Describe one of your classmates.
3. Play a game! One student says I'm thinking of someone in the class. The other students must ask him questions to try to guess who he's thinking of.

Complete the following dialogue — you can do it alone or with a group of students.

Sam: Where are you from?

Chan: I'm from Cambodia.

Sam: Cambodia! Where's Cambodia?

Chan: _____

Sam: _____

Chan: _____

Sam: _____

11.
A New Schedule

I study English every day. My class starts at 9 a.m. I always get up early, about 6:30 a.m., and eat breakfast. I usually have rice, pork and eggs. I'm used to eating Lao food. I'm not used to American food. After breakfast, I wash up and get ready for school.

This morning I got a phone call. It was from the employment office. They have a job for me. It's a janitor's job. I'll be working nights. My hours are from 6 p.m. to midnight. I start tomorrow. I'm lucky; I can go to school during the day and work at night.

Now I'll be busy all the time. I'll have a busy schedule. It will be nice to make some money.

Review Vocabulary	New Vocabulary
phone call	breakfast
employment agency	eggs
job	pork
busy	janitor
since	midnight
	tomorrow
	schedule
	money

Review Verbs	New Verbs
study	
eat	get up
get	be used to
start	wash up
Past Tense	start
left	
Review Expressions	
all the time	

49

<u>True, False, or Maybe</u> — If the answer is true, write "T".
If the answer is false, write "F".
If the answer is maybe, write "M".

1. Sitha studies at night. _____
2. Sitha gets up early. _____
3. He never eats breakfast. _____
4. He got a phone call from the restaurant. _____
5. Sitha is a busy man. _____
6. He likes to be busy. _____

Questions — Answer the following questions.
1. What does Sitha study?
2. What does he eat for breakfast?
3. What do you eat for breakfast?
4. What kind of a job did Sitha get?
5. Is it a good job?
6. Would you like to be a janitor?

Tell Me.
1. What's Sitha's schedule?

a. _____

b. _____

c. _____

2. What's your schedule?

a. _____

b. _____

c. _____

d. _____

Grammar Practice — Change the following sentences into questions. Use one of the following question words whenever possible.

when	where
what time	who
how	why
how many	

1. I always get up early.
2. I usually get up at 6:30 in the morning.
3. My working hours are from 6 p.m. to midnight.
4. I'll be working nights.
5. I'll have a busy schedule.

Just for fun — complete the following story, using your own words.

I study _____. I study from _____ to _____.
         (subject)   (what time)   (what time)

I study for _____. I always get up at _____. I
       (how many hours)   (what time)

eat _____ for breakfast. After I eat breakfast I _____
   (name of food)

_____
                   (do what?)

_____

_____

_____

_____.

A Busy Day

Directions:

First answer all of the questions yourself and then ask a class-mate the same questions. Write down his or her answers.

Your Name _____ Your Neighbor's Name _____

	You:	Your Neighbor:
1. What time do you get up every morning?		
2. What do you eat for breakfast?		
3. What do you do after breakfast?		
4. What do you eat for lunch?		
5. What do you do in your spare time?		
6. Where do you work and/or study?		
7. How do you get to work or school?		
8. How do you feel at the end of the day?		

12.
My New Job

I'm a janitor in the local High School. I work with two other men. One man is from Haiti and the other is from Hong Kong. The Haitian man is a refugee, like me. His name is Enrique. The man from Hong Kong is an immigrant. His name is Lin Fong. None of us can speak English very well but we all practice with each other.

My boss is American. His name is Joe White. He speaks very quickly. Sometimes he gets angry when we don't understand him. I'm not afraid of him. I just ask him to speak slowly. When he's not angry, he's very nice. Sometimes he even kids around with us.

At 7:30 we get a dinner break. My boss goes to a restaurant to eat dinner. I want to save money. I bring dinner from home, and Enrique and Lin Fong do too. For dinner I usually eat rice, vegetables and pork. Lin Fong eats rice and pork too. Enrique eats fish and rice for dinner. Joe always tells us what he ate in the restaurant. He usually has soup, steak, potatoes and a salad. I'm used to eating a lot of rice. I really don't like potatoes.

Lin Fong, Enrique and I are good friends. Lin Fong wants me to meet his family. He's married and has three kids. Enrique is a single man like me. On Sunday, Enrique and I will go to Lin Fong's house for lunch. It's nice to have friends.

Review Vocabulary

week
janitor
Hong Kong
refugee
just
afraid
nice
pork
Sunday

New Vocabulary

local
high school
Haiti
none
quick
angry
dinner
break
restaurant

vegetables
soup
steak
potatoes
salad
lunch
kids
immigrant

Review Verbs and Verb Phrases

work
speak
practice
ask
joke
eat
want

tell
have
go
meet
be used to
boss

New Verbs and Verb Phrases

save
kid around

<u>True, False, or Maybe</u> — If the answer is true, write "T".
If the answer is false, write "F".
If the answer is maybe, write "M".

1. Sitha is a dishwasher in a restaurant. _____
2. He works with two Cuban men. _____
3. The men he works with can speak English very well. _____
4. Sitha eats dinner with his boss. _____
5. Sitha doesn't like American food. _____

Questions — Answer the following questions.
1. What does Sitha do?
2. Who does he work with?
3. What does Sitha usually eat for dinner?
4. What do you usually eat for dinner?

For Advanced Students

1. What is the difference between an immigrant and a refugee?

Tell Me.

1. Tell me about Sitha's boss.

   a. _____

   b. _____

2. Tell me about your boss. (If you're not working, tell me about your boss in your native country.)

   a. _____

   b. _____

   c. _____

3. What do you eat for breakfast, lunch and dinner?

breakfast	lunch	dinner
a. _____	a. _____	a. _____
b. _____	b. _____	b. _____

Grammar Practice — When we put "be used to" in front of a <u>verb</u>, we change the <u>verb</u> to the 'ing' form.

example: I'm not used to drinking coffee.
I'm not used to drinking milk.

Make your own sentences using "be used to" and include one of the following words in each sentence.

1. cold water
2. his teacher
3. baseball
4. hot weather
5. football
6. the park

Example: I am used to cold water. **or:**

I'm used to swimming in cold water.

1. _____

2. _____

3. _____

4. _____

5. _____

6. _____

Grammar Practice — Change the following sentences to include "be used to".

example: I study in the morning.
I am used to studying in the morning.

1. He works in the evening.

_____

2. They eat rice for dinner.

_____

3. She doesn't eat lunch.

_____

4. He doesn't get up early.

_____

5. We get a dinner break at 7:30.

_____

6. Joe eats dinner in a restaurant.

_____

Just for fun — Answer the following question.
Tell me five things that you're used to doing.

1. _____

2. _____

3. _____

4. _____

5. _____

13.
The Robbery

I was coming back from work. It was after midnight. I was waiting for a bus on the corner of 28th Street. There wasn't anyone else around. Suddenly a man came over to me. He was very tall and had blond hair, a brown beard and moustache, and brown eyes. He looked around, then he asked, "Do you have a match?" "Sure," I said. I gave him a book of matches. Suddenly he took out a gun and said, "Give me your money."

I was so nervous I didn't know what to do. I couldn't think in English. I started to speak Lao. The thief said, "Hey man, I don't understand Spanish, just give me your money." I gave him all my money. He ran away quickly.

Now I was really scared. I wasn't sure what to do. I felt so alone. Suddenly a young couple walked by. I said to them, "I was just robbed." They told me to go to the police. Luckily, there was a police station around the corner.

Review Vocabulary		New Vocabulary	
midnight	eyes	after	gun
bus	just	suddenly	nervous
corner	Spanish	beard	couple
anyone	quick	moustache	police
around	really	brown	police station
blonde	scared	match	tall
hair	luckily	box	rob
		sure	else

Review Verbs

wait	know
have	think
give	

New Verbs

looked around	rob
take out	

New Expressions

hey man

True, False, or Maybe — If the answer is true, write "T".
If the answer is false, write "F".
If the answer is maybe, write "M".

1. Sitha was coming home from school. _____
2. The man asked Sitha for the time. _____
3. The man was afraid. _____
4. The man thought Sitha was Cuban. _____
5. The police station was nearby. _____

Questions — Answer the following questions.
1. What was Sitha doing when he got robbed?
2. What time did Sitha get robbed?
3. What did the thief look like?
4. How did Sitha feel when he got robbed?
5. Why was Sitha unable to speak English?
6. Why did the thief think Sitha was speaking Spanish?

Vocabulary Practice — Read this story over again. Complete the following sentences using the correct expression.

looked around   took out
hey man   walk by
come back   come over

1. I _____ for my friend, but I didn't see him.

2. The thief _____ a gun.

3. _____, how are you doing?

4. Can you _____ my house at 6:00?

5. Sorry you have to go. Please _____ soon.

6. On my way to work I _____ the school.

14.

At the Police Station

The police station was very crowded. The policemen were very busy. Many phones were ringing. There was a lot of noise and confusion. I looked around for someone who wasn't busy.

There was a lady waiting to see the police too. She said, "These cops don't pay attention to anyone. I've waited here one hour already. They just tell me to be patient and wait my turn."

I also had to wait and wait and wait.

Finally —

Policeman:	What's your problem?
Sitha:	I was robbed.
Policeman:	Can you describe the thief?
Sitha:	Sure.
Policeman:	Are you sure you can describe him?
Sitha:	Yes, of course.
Policeman:	What did the thief steal?
Sitha:	He stole my money.
Policeman:	How much money did he steal?
Sitha:	Thirty dollars.
Policeman:	Okay, fill out this form. Make sure to describe the thief. Write the exact location and time of the robbery. Give all the details.
Sitha:	I'll try. It's difficult to remember everything.
Policeman:	We'll try to find the thief, but don't count on it.
Sitha:	It sure is dangerous to be out alone at night.
Policeman:	Yes, you're lucky you only lost some money and not your life.

Review Vocabulary		New Vocabulary
police station	life	policemen
busy	police	cops
noise	hour	exact
phones	turn	location
only	finally	details
money	problem	everywhere
		already

Review Verbs and Expressions		New Verbs and Verb Phrases	
ring	had to	make sure	describe
talk	look around	count on something	steal
wait	of course	be out	be patient
try	fill out	**Present Perfect Tense**	
remember	get robbed	have waited	
find			

True, False, or Maybe — If the answer is true, write "T".

If the answer is false, write "F".

If the answer is maybe, write "M".

1. The police station was noisy. _____
2. Sitha had to wait a long time. _____
3. He had to fill out a form. _____
4. Sitha couldn't describe the thief. _____
5. The police will find the thief. _____

Questions — Answer the following questions.

1. Describe the police station.
2. How much money did the thief steal?
3. What was the location and time of the robbery?
4. Do you think Sitha was lucky? Why?
5. Is it dangerous to be out alone at night where you live? Why?

Vocabulary — Fill in each blank using the correct expression.

be patient   count on
make sure   be out

1. I'm afraid to _____ alone at night.

2. You can usually _____ your friends to help you.

3. _____ you know where you are going.

4. I'll help you soon, please _____.

Create your own dialogue — You can do this alone or with a group of students.
You've just been robbed. Go to the police and report the robbery.

You: I was just robbed!

Policeman: _____.

You   _____.

Policeman: _____.

You: _____.

Just for fun — Answer the following questions.
1. What happens to thieves in your country?
2. Tell me about a time that you were robbed.

Read the following situations. In your opinion, do you think that one of the characters is a thief? Why do you think so?

1. Som is walking down a dark street. There is no one around. Two men come out of an old building. They are whispering to each other. One man walks to the corner. The other man approaches Som and asks him for directions.
   What do you think? Is this man a thief? Why? What should Som do?

2. Ning is on the subway. She is carrying a purse. The man sitting across from her is staring at her purse. He is very young, maybe seventeen or eighteen. His clothes are old· and he looks poor. He gets off the subway at the same stop as Ning.
   What do you think? Is this young man a thief? Why? What should Ning do?

3. Charles wants to buy a ring for his girlfriend Maria. He goes into a big jewelry store. The salesman shows him a small gold ring with an emerald stone. The ring is very expensive, but the gold doesn't shine and the emerald has many scratches on it. Charles doesn't really like the ring, but the salesman insists that he buy it. The salesman tells Charles that the ring is of excellent quality.
   What do you think? Is the salesman a thief? Is he being honest with Charles? Should Charles buy the ring? What should he do?

15.
Buying Clothes

It's almost winter. It's getting cold. I'm not used to cold weather, but I hope I'll get used to it. I'm looking forward to seeing snow. I've never seen snow. It never snows in Laos. Laos has a warm climate.

I have to buy winter clothes. I need a winter coat, sweaters, heavy pants, gloves, a scarf and a hat. Clothes are expensive, and I don't have much money. I'll have to buy my winter wardrobe little by little.

Today I'm going shopping at the department store. There's a sale on wool sweaters. I don't know what size I take. I hope the salesman will help me.

In the Department Store

Sitha:	Where's the men's department?
Salesgirl I:	On the 3rd floor. Take the escalator up.

On the 3rd floor.

Sitha:	Is this the men's department?
Salesgirl II:	No! The men's department is over there, behind the shoe department.

Salesman:	Can I help you?
Sitha:	Yes, I want to buy a sweater.
Salesman:	What size do you wear?
Sitha:	I'm not sure. A small size.
Salesman:	Yes, you Cuban people are small.
Sitha:	I'm not Cuban. I'm from Laos. Laotians are small people too.
Salesman:	Here's a size 34. Try it on.
Sitha:	It fits, but I don't like the color. Do you have green?
Salesman:	No, this is the only color we have in stock.
Sitha:	Oh! That's too bad. I really need a sweater.
Salesman:	We'll try the Boy's department. They have small sizes there.
Sitha:	What a good idea!

Review Vocabulary

cold
really
clothes
money
Cuban

New Vocabulary

snow	almost
climate	expensive
winter coat	department (dept.)
sweater	floor
heavy pants	escalator
gloves	shoe
scarf	size
hat	green
color	stock

Review Verbs

get	help
like	buy
see	wear
take	need

New Verbs and Verb Phrases
Present Tense

hope	look forward to
fit	try on

Present Perfect Tense

have seen

Review Expression

a good idea

New Expressions

over there
that's too bad

<u>True, False, or Maybe</u> — If the answer is true, write "T".
If the answer is false, write "F".
If the answer is maybe, write "M".

1. It's November. _____
2. Sitha is used to cold weather. _____
3. It often snows in Laos. _____
4. Sitha is rich. _____
5. The men's department is on the third floor. _____

Questions — Answer the following questions.
1. What's the climate like in Boston in the wintertime?
2. How did Sitha get to the third floor of the department store?
3. What size sweater do you wear?
4. What's your favorite color?
5. What color does Sitha like?

Vanishing Dialogue — Read the dialogue in this story again. Fill in each blank with the correct word. Try not to look back at the story.

Sitha: Where's the _____ _____?

Salesgirl: On the 3rd _____, take the _____ up.

Sitha: (on the 3rd floor) _____ the men's department?

Salesgirl: The ___ ___ is _____ the shoe department.

Salesman: Can I _____ you?

Sitha: Yes, I _____ ___ _____ a sweater.

Salesman: What _____ do you _____?

Sitha: I'm not _____, a _____ size.

Salesman: Yes, you _____ people are _____.

Sitha: I'm not _____. I'm from _____.

Salesman: Here's a _____ 34. _____ it on.

Sitha: It _____, but I don't like the _____.

            Do you have _____ _____?

Salesman: No, this is the _____ color we have in _____.

Sitha: Oh, _____ _____ _____ I really need a sweater.

Salesman: Well, _____ the boy's _____. They

            have small _____ there.

Sitha: What a _____ _____!

Just for fun — For Advanced Students
1. Describe your favorite article of clothing.
2. How did men and women dress in your native country?
   How do American men and women dress?
   Which do you like better?
3. Tell me what you'd wear in the following situations.
   a. Going to a job interview. You are interviewing to be a
      waiter in a fancy French restaurant.
   b. It's snowing out, you're going out with your friend to
      have a snowball fight.
   c. You are going out to eat in a fancy restaurant.
   d. You are going to visit your friend.
   e. You have an appointment with the doctor.
   f. You are going on a picnic.
   g. You are going to the beach.
   h. It's very cold out, maybe it will rain. You are going for a
      walk.
   i. You are going skiing in the mountains.
   j. You are going hiking in the mountains. It is a beautiful
      spring day.

67

4. Where would you buy the following things?
   a. winter clothes
   b. ski clothes
   c. skis
   d. a bathing suit
   e. sunglasses
   f. hiking boots
   g. tennis shoes
   h. a tennis racket
   i. boots for the snow

5. What size shoes do you wear?
   What size dress do you wear?
   What size hat do you wear?
   What size socks do you wear?
   What size gloves do you wear?
   What size bra do you wear?
   What size underwear do you wear?
   What size shirt do you wear?
   What size skirt do you wear?
   What size pants do you wear?
   What size ring do you wear?
   What size blouse do you wear?
   What size coat do you wear?
   What's your height?
   What's your weight?

6. What would you do in the following situations?

   a. Your sponsor bought you a sweater. You really don't like the color and the sweater's too big for you. What should you do?

   b. You bought a new pair of shoes. You wore them for one day and they gave you terrible blisters. What can you do?

   c. You bought a new dress on sale. Your husband didn't like it and thought that it was too expensive. He wants you to return it. Can you? Do you have the receipt? Must you listen to your husband?

Spring

Summer

69

Fall

Winter

16.
Money

I didn't buy anything in the department store. On my way home, I saw a good-looking sweater in the window of a small clothing store. I went in and tried the sweater on. It fit very well. It wasn't too expensive. The price tag said $15.99. I took the sweater to the cashier. She asked me for $17.11. "But the price is $15.99," I said. "You must pay 7% sales tax," she said. "All together, the sweater costs $17.11."

I always get confused when I use American money. The name of American money is dollars. The name of the money in Laos is kip. Each dollar bill has one hundred cents. There are coins also. Each coin has a different value. A penny is one cent, a nickel is five cents, a dime is ten cents, a quarter is twenty-five cents and a half dollar is fifty cents. It's very confusing.

I gave the cashier 3 five dollar bills, two one's, two dimes and one penny. She took the money and counted it. Then she gave me back one dime. "You gave me too much," she said. "Two dimes and a penny are twenty-one cents, not eleven cents. Be careful with your money or you might get ripped off."

I always get my dimes and nickles mixed up. A dime is smaller than a nickle but it's worth more. I hope I don't make that mistake again. Next time I may not get an honest cashier.

penny   dime   half dollar

nickle   quarter

Review Vocabulary	New Vocabulary	
department store	price tag	value
sweater	cashier	penny (1¢)
store	price	nickel (5¢)
expensive	percent (%)	dime (10¢)
confused	sales tax	quarter (25¢)
money	mistake	half dollar (50¢)
	window	one dollar ($1.00)
	beautiful	

Review Verbs
buy
fit
give
hope

window
beautiful
dollars ($)
kip
cents (¢)
coins

Past Tense
saw
went
gave
tried
took

**New Verbs
and Verb Phrases**

pay
use
may
ripped off
get mixed up
be worth
next time
be careful

True, False, or Maybe — If the answer is true, write "T".
                                                    If the answer is false, write "F".
                                                    If the answer is maybe, write "M".

1. Sitha had to pay $15.99 for the sweater. _____
2. Sitha gave the cashier too much money. _____
3. The cashier gave Sitha his money back. _____
4. Sitha felt very foolish. _____
5. A nickel is worth more than a dime. _____

Questions — Answer the following questions.
1. How much money did Sitha give the cashier?
2. Was it the correct amount?
3. Which coins did Sitha get confused?
4. What does the word "honest" mean?
5. Which is bigger, a nickel or a dime? Which is worth more?

Vocabulary Practice — Read stories 15 and 16 again. Fill in each blank using the correct expression.

     try on   mixed up   looking forward
     worth   next time

1. I'm _____ to seeing my family.

2. Can I _____ this sweater?

3. It's a beautiful sweater, but it's not _____ $50.00.

4. You look like your sister. I always get you _____ .

5. Sorry, _____ I won't make the same mistake.

Money Review
    Let's review American money.
    What is the name of the paper money?_____

    The names of the coins are _____

Fill in the following chart.

Name of Coin	Value of Coin
1. _Penny_	1. _one cent — 1¢_
2. _____	2. _____
3. _____	3. _____
4. _____	4. _____
5. _____	5. _____

How many pennies are there in one dollar? _____

How many nickels are there in one dollar? _____

How many dimes are there in one dollar? _____

How many quarters are there in one dollar? _____

How many half dollars are there in one dollar? _____

The money game: Play this game with your classmates.
Materials needed: Two boxes filled with coins, one die
                  Lots of smart, quick students!
Directions: 1. Break the class into two teams.
                  2. Roll the die, the number on the die is the
                     number of points the winner will get.
                  3. The teacher (or fellow student) calls out:
                     "give me 48 cents"
                  4. 2 members from each team come up. The
                     first person to give the teacher the correct
                     amount of change is the winner. His team
                     gets the point.

                  The different language that can be used is:

                  Give me _____ cents.
                  Give me 5 quarters, 3 dimes, 4 nickles, 10
                  pennies.

                  You have a dollar to by something for 83 cents.
                  How much change do you get? The person
                  who gives you the right amount of change is
                  the winner.

17.

House Hunting

I live with a Laotian family. There are many people living in the house. It's very crowded. I'd like to move out and rent a small apartment, but I don't want to live alone. Enrique, my Haitian friend, is also looking for an apartment. Maybe we can live together as roommates. Rents are very expensive in the city. I hope I can find a cheap apartment to rent.

I read the newspaper all the time. There are many apartments for rent advertised in the paper. They're all expensive. There is a real estate agency in my neighborhood. He said he could find me an apartment, but that I would have to pay him! I don't know if it's worth it. How do I know that he's an honest man? Can I count on him? Will he rip me off?

I hope I can find an apartment soon. I'm looking forward to getting my own place.

Review Vocabulary		**New Vocabulary**	
alone	expensive	roommates	realtor
cheap	honest	apartment	cheap
newspaper	Haitian	real estate agency	
	neighborhood		

Review Verbs		**New Verbs**
live	read	rent
look	help	move out
find	pay	
hope	rip off	

<u>True, False, or Maybe</u> — If the answer is true, write "T".
If the answer is false, write "F".
If the answer is maybe, write "M".

1. Sitha wants to live alone. _____
2. Enrique will be Sitha's roommate. _____
3. The realtor isn't an honest man. _____
4. Sitha is looking forward to moving out. _____
5. He'll find an apartment from the ads in the paper. _____

Questions — Answer the following questions.
1. Why is Sitha looking forward to getting his own apartment?
2. Are rents cheap in Boston?
3. Who does Sitha want to live with?
4. Why do you think he doesn't want to live alone?
5. Do you want to live alone? Why?

Tell Me.
1. Tell me about the people you live with.

   a. _____

   b. _____

   c. _____

2. Tell me about your house in your native country.

   a. _____

   b. _____

   c. _____

Grammar Review — Use the past tense form of each of the following words in an original sentence.

1. live		6. advertise	
2. look		7. speak	
3. find		8. help	
4. hope		9. pay	
5. read			

1. _____

2. _____

3. _____

4. _____

5. _____

6. _____

7. _____

8. _____

9. _____

Complete the following dialogue.

Sitha: I found a nice apartment for rent. Would you like to share it with me?

Enrique: Well, I don't know. I'd have to see it. I want to make sure we're not getting ripped off.

Sitha: _____

Enrique: _____

18.

Apartment For Rent

There are many apartment houses in my neighborhood. On the way home from school, I saw a sign on one of them. It was on the front door. It said, Apartments for Rent, Inquire Within. I stopped in and spoke to the superintendent. He showed me an apartment on the fifth floor. It was a one bedroom apartment. It had a kitchen, a living room, a bedroom and a bathroom. There wasn't any furniture in the apartment. One window was broken. I spoke to the superintendent about the apartment.

Sitha:	How much is the rent?
Super:	$350.00 a month.
Sitha:	That's expensive for me.
Super:	We'll paint the apartment for you. We'll also repair the broken window.
Sitha:	It's still expensive, do you have something cheaper?
Super:	There's a cheaper apartment on the ground floor.
Sitha:	I'd like to see it.

The ground floor apartment had one bedroom, a kitchen, a small living room and a tiny bathroom. There was a stove and refrigerator in the kitchen. The apartment had some furniture: an old couch and chair in the living room.

Super:	The rent here is $275.00 a month. You have to sign a year's lease and leave a $100.00 cleaning deposit.
Sitha:	I'd like to think about it first. I want to talk to my friend. He wants to share the apartment with me. He'll want to come see it too.
Super:	Okay, think it over. It doesn't matter to me. Lots of people want apartments these days.

Review Vocabulary

apartment house
neighborhood
floor
rent
window
still
expensive
cheaper

New Vocabulary

kitchen	sign
stove	inquire
refrigerator	within
couch	superintendent (super)
chair	bedroom
furniture	living room
lease	bathroom
cleaning deposit	door

Review Verbs and Verb Phrases

rent
leave
make sure

Past Tense

spoke

Review Expressions

it doesn't matter

New Verbs and Verb Phrases

share
sign
think something over

Past Tense

ripped off
showed

Just for fun

1. Describe your favorite room in your house.
2. Pick a room in your house. Describe the different furniture and appliances in that room. Tell me what each thing is used for.

Example:	Room	Appliance or Furniture	Use
	kitchen	stove	We cook on the stove.
	kitchen	table	We eat at the table.

Draw a room in a house. It can be any room. How are you going to decorate it? What are you going to put on the walls? What color will the room be? What furniture are you going to put in the room? Draw the picture in the space below. Write the names of all the furniture, appliances and decorations that you draw in the picture.

19.

Meeting the Neighbors

Enrique and I now share the ground floor apartment. We're happy living there. Enrique is a good roommate. He's honest, neat and clean. We get along well. Enrique has a lot of friends. They often stop in and visit. We bought some second hand furniture; a table, four chairs and a lamp. I always look forward to coming home to my new apartment.

I was coming home one day when I met my neighbor. Her name is Susan. She stopped to speak with me in the hall.

Susan: Hi! How long have you lived here?
Sitha: Not too long, about a month.
Susan: Oh, I haven't seen you around.
Sitha: Well, I've only lived here a month.
Susan: Who do you live with?
Sitha: My friend Enrique, we work together. Who do you live with?
Susan: I live alone.
Sitha: Don't you get lonely?
Susan: Sometimes. Would you like to come in and have a cup of coffee?
Sitha: Okay.
Susan: Sit down. I'll make some coffee.
Sitha: Thank you. You have a nice apartment.
Susan: I used to live here with my husband. He fixed up the apartment. Now we are divorced. Are you married?
Sitha: No, but I'd like to get married.
Susan: Do you have a girlfriend?
Sitha: I used to have one, but not now.
Susan: What do you do?
Sitha: I'm a janitor.

Susan:	I'm a secretary. I hate it! I'm thinking of going back to school. I'd like to take up nursing.
Sitha:	I'm studying English now. I'd like to go to college someday.
Susan:	Your English is pretty good. Listen, there's a good movie playing in the neighborhood. Do you want to go see it?
Sitha:	Uh — I'm not sure. I have to think it over.
Susan:	Well, think quickly. The movie starts in an hour!

Review Vocabulary

roommate	together
honest	alone
neat	lonely
clean	yet
table	janitor
chairs	neighborhood
lamp	quickly
apartment	hour

Review Expressions

get along
stop in
look forward to
be sure
think something over

Review Verbs

share	play
visit	start
sit	

Past Tense

bought
met
lived

New Vocabulary

second-hand
cup
coffee
girlfriend
secretary (sec'y)
someday
pretty
movie
hall
nursing

New Verbs and Verb Phrases

hate
see someone around
be divorced
fix up
take up

Past Tense

used to

Questions — Answer the following questions.
1. Do you think Sitha likes Susan? Why?
2. Do you think Susan is lonely? Why?
3. Do you think Susan likes Sitha? Why?
4. Do you think Sitha will go to the movies with Susan?

Vanishing Dialogue — Read the dialogue in this story again. Fill in each blank with the correct word. Try not to look back at the story.

Susan: Hi, _____ have you _____ here?

Sitha: Not _____ long _____ a month.

Susan: Oh, I haven't _____ you _____ much.

Sitha: Well, I've only _____ here a _____.

Susan: _____ do you _____ with?

Sitha: My friend Enrique, we work _____. Who do

you _____ with?

Susan: I live _____.

Sitha: Don't you get lonely?

Susan: _____. Would you _____ to come _____

and have a _____ of coffee?

Sitha: _____.

Susan: Sit _____, I'll _____ some coffee.

Sitha: Thank you. You _____ a nice _____.

Susan: I __ __ __ here with my husband. Now we're

_____. He ____ ____ up the apartment. Are

you married?

Sitha: No, but I'd _____ to get _____.

Susan: Do you have a _____?

Sitha: No, _____ . I used to have one, but _____ _____.

Susan: What _____ you _____?

Sitha: I'm a _____.

Susan: I'm a _____. I _____ it. I'm _____ of

_____ back to school.

Sitha: I'm _____ English now. I'd like to go to _____

someday.

Susan: Your English is _____ good. Listen, there's a

_____ movie playing in the _____. Do

you want to ____ ____ it?

Sitha: Uh - I'm ____ ____. I have to _____ it _____

Susan: Well, think _____, the movie _____ in

an _____.

Just For Fun

For the girls in the class — Answer the following questions.
1. Do you like American men? Why?
2. How are American men different than men in your country?
3. Do you like Susan? Why?
4. Do ladies in your country live alone?
5. In your culture, if a woman is attracted to a man, how does she act?
6. Describe some of the differences between American women and women from your country.

For the men in the class — Answer the following questions.
1. Do you like American women? Why?
2. How are they different than women in your native country?
3. Do you like Susan? Why?
4. In your culture, if a woman is attracted to a man, how does she act?
5. What is women's liberation?

20.

My Greatest Accomplishment

My English teacher asked each student in the class to write a composition titled "The Greatest Accomplishment of My Life."

I'm not sure what to write about. I've thought it over for a long time. I did many things in the past year. Leaving Laos and swimming across the Mekhong river were accomplishments. Coming to America, getting a job, going to school and meeting new people were all accomplishments.

All in all, I think my greatest accomplishment was learning English. I still make many mistakes. Sometimes I don't understand everything people are saying, but each day I get better and better.

I told my teacher that this was a difficult composition to write. After all, it's hard to measure everything you've done in your life.

Review Expressions

think something over
be sure
get a job

Review Vocabulary

pretty

Review Verb
Past Tense

asked

New Vocabulary
and New Expressions

composition
title
great
accomplishment
mistakes
titled
all in all
after all

New Verbs
measure

Present Perfect
have thought

Just for fun

Now you've read many stories about Sitha.
1. Do you like him?
2. Does he remind you of yourself? Why?
3. Were your experiences similar?
4. What do you think Sitha's greatest accomplishment was? What is yours?
5. What do you think the future holds for Sitha?
6. What do you think the future holds for you?

Now that you've read Sitha's story, it's time to write your own. Start now on the next few pages . . .

Good Luck!

My Story

_____

_____

_____

_____

_____

_____

_____

_____

_____

_____

_____

_____

Teaching Suggestions for lesson 1

1. Have students write or tell about their hometown. This can be done with Silent-Way Rods. The students can "build" their hometown with the Rods.
2. Divide into groups and have the groups compare city life to country life.
3. Divide the class into groups and have them list the different things they can do in the country and the city.
4. Have students answer the following: "If I could live anywhere in the world, I'd live in _____."

Teaching Suggestions for lesson 2

1. Have the students describe a friend of theirs.
2. Have the students write a letter to a friend in another country.
3. Have students continue this story and have Lee Pao and Sitha meet in America.
4. Have students pair up with one another and have them find out about each other's culture by filling out a form similar to the one below.

Custom	Student A	Student B
	Name _____ Name _____	
	Native	Native
	Country _____ Country _____	
	Describe how it is done in your country.	
Food		
Dress		
Marriage		
Education		
Religion		
Sports		

5. Have students pair up with each other and have them create a dialogue. The subject: Two good friends speaking to each other.

Teaching Suggestions for lesson 4

1. Use the following list (or create your own) and have the students tell you how they obtained these things in their native country and how they'll obtain them in America.

	NATIVE COUNTRY	AMERICA
Rice		
Sugar		
Milk		
Bananas		
Clothes		
House		
Shoes		
Furniture		
Medicine		
Education		

2. Have a "trade-in". Give each students a few possessions. Then give them a need. Have them trade their unwanted or unneeded possessions for their specific need.

3. List things found in a supermarket then teach the classifying nouns that go with each item.
   Example

   A <u>bottle</u> of aspirin
   A <u>can</u> of beans
   A <u>bag</u> of sugar.

Teaching Suggestions for lesson 5

1. Make a list of different ways to communicate. (phone, mail, etc.)
2. Bring a phone into class and have students role play the situation in this story.
3. Discuss what Sitha should have done next.
4. Play the telephone game and other communication games.
5. Using the telephone try various telephone situations:
   Calling the hospital because your wife is giving birth.
   Calling the police station because your house was robbed.
   Calling a friend to invite him to a party.
6. Discuss local phone calls, long distance phone calls, operator assisted phone calls, station to station calls, person to person calls and collect calls. Using a phone have students practice making all of these different calls.

Teaching Suggestions for lesson 6

1. Have students tell about their occupations in their native country and what they would like to do in America.
2. Break class up into groups, make a list of all different ways that people find jobs. Have groups compare lists.
3. Bring in the classified section of a newspaper. Have students read it and choose a job that they feel qualified for. Teach want ad vocabulary. Break students up into groups, have them create their own job ads using new vocabulary.
4. Give each student an occupation. Have him discuss what the "occupation" does, location of the job, job responsibilities and qualifications needed for each job.

Teaching Suggestions for lesson 7

1. Have a mock job interview with competition. Have two students interview for the same job. Have the class decide which student is the best qualified for the job. Have them state reasons why.
2. Have students fill out a real job application. (It's okay to copy p. 32.)
3. Break into groups, have students discuss what is proper to wear for a job interview. (Would they choose the same clothes for a different job?)

Teaching Suggestions for lesson 8

1. Break class into pairs, have each pair create a dialogue between an employer and prospective employee.
2. Distribute job advertisements from the newspaper to the class. Have them decipher the ads and write down the name of the job, responsibilities of the job, qualifications needed, educational requirements and where to apply for the job.
3. Ask students if they could have any job, what job they would choose to have.
4. Distribute as many different job application forms as you can find. Have students practice filling them out.
5. Discuss fringe benefits that some jobs offer.
6. Divide class into two groups, one group has just gotten a new job, the other group has just been rejected for a job that they applied for. Have them list the emotions that they feel, teacher can work with these emotions in various ways, using role playing, dialogue writing, and discussion.

Teaching Suggestions for lesson 10

1. Tell each student to write a description of the student sitting next to him.
2. Bring in pictures of people from different countries and have students describe them. Discuss similarities and differences between the people. Then have students guess what country the people are from.
3. Discuss preconceived ideas people have of different ethnic groups.
4. Bring in a world map and do map work.
5. Teacher describes a certain type of person and have students guess where he or she is from.
6. Break class into groups, have them make a list of countries. Have students write the nationality and the language that the people of each country speak.

Example	Country	Nationality	Language
	Cuba	Cuban	Spanish

7. Using the list from exercise number 6, hand each student a piece of paper with the name of a country on it. Tell the students that now they come from that country. They must walk around the room and meet all the people from different countries and start a conversation with them.

Teaching Suggestions for lessons 11 and 12

1. Make a list of daily activities in student's native country and their daily activities in America. Compare the differences.
2. Have a discussion on diet and dietary habits in different cultures.
3. Have the students answer the following questions:
   What meals are usually eaten with the family?
   How many times a day did you eat in your native country?
   Who prepares the family meals in your family?
   Do you often eat away from home? Why?
   What foods are especially healthy?
   What are your favorite foods?
4. Have student keep a journal of their daily activities.
5. Make a list of things people like to do in their spare time.
6. Have each student tell of one funny experience that they've had since arriving in America.

Teaching Suggestions for lessons 13 and 14

1. Discuss how thieves are punished in different cultures.
2. ave a discussion about "Crime in America," and have students compare it to crime in their native country.
3. Role play situations where students must report an accident, crime, robbery or fight to the police.
4. Discuss different laws in America and compare them with the laws in the students' native country. Example, in Laos it's legal for Hmongs to have more than one wife, in America it isn't legal.
5. There are many idiomatic expressions in this story. Go over the meaning of each expression and have students create sentences using these expressions.
6. Have students create their own dialogues, topics can be
   1. Reporting a crime
   2. Getting robbed
   3. It is illegal

Teaching Suggestions for lesson 15

1. Talk about different seasons in different countries.
2. Display landscape or scenery pictures depicting different seasons. Have the class describe the pictures and guess which season each depicts.
3. Discuss clothing needed for each season. Have students tell how they dressed in the different seasons in their native country.
4. Make a list of activities and have students tell which season they are performed in. This can be a group activity.
5. Have a geography lesson using a world map. Discuss the different weather which occurs in different parts of the world.
6. List the variety of emotions felt during a bad storm. Have the students write their own stories using the emotions from the list.
7. Make a Question Box. Have each student interview a classmate asking him or her various questions about is or her favorite season.

Teaching Suggestions for lesson 16

1. Working with money, set up a store in the classroom. Give people the role of salesperson and customer. Have them buy items, pay, ask for change, etc.
2. Give each student a certain amount of money. Break class into groups and make a list of things that they want to buy. The list can consist of food, clothing, or appliances. Put the completed list on the board. Then ask students where they would buy these things, and how much they think it would cost. When place and price are set, have students budget their money and buy the things that they want to buy.
3. Game — Call two students to the board. Call out a price ex. ($1.98). The first student who can write it correctly on the board gets a point. First student to get five points is the winner.
4. Have students create a dialogue using monetary terms. Teacher can supply the terms to be used in the dialogue.

Teaching Suggestions for lessons 17 and 18

1. Have students draw pictures of their houses in their native country, and in the refugee camp or America. (depending on where they are living at present moment) Discuss and compare similarities and differences between the houses.
2. Have students write about their "Dream House".
3. Bring in toy model furniture and have students explain its function in the house.
4. Have each student choose a room in a house and thoroughly describe an activity that is carried out in that room (i.e. kitchen — preparing food, cooking, washing dishes, eating meals, storing food, etc.)
5. Role Play — an encounter between landlord and househunter. Direct conversation to include price, terms of lease, number of rooms, etc.
6. Show pictures of private homes and apartment houses. Elicit discussion on the relative merits of each. Where would the students prefer to live? Why?

Teaching Suggestions for lesson 19

1. Have your students role play the following situations:
   a. Your beautiful young neighbor comes to your house to borrow a cup of sugar.
   b. The woman sitting next to you in English class asks you to drive her home.
   c. You've been dating a man for 2 months and you find out that he is married. You now must confront him with this information.
   d. You go to the movies with a young man that you met at work, he asks you to pay for your own ticket.
2. Discuss women's roles in today's society and in different cultures.
3. Discuss how American women are different than women in your students' native country.
4. Discuss marriage customs and divorce.
5. Have students change the ending of this story.
6. Discuss appropriate body language in different cultures.